Getting Ready

A Career as a Computer Animator

by Bill Lund

Content Consultant:
Howard Green, Director of Studio Communications
Walt Disney Studios

CAPSTONE PRESS
MANKATO, MINNESOTA

C A P S T O N E   P R E S S

818 North Willow Street • Mankato, Minnesota 56001
http://www.capstone-press.com

Library of Congress Cataloging-in-Publication Data
Lund, Bill, 1954-
Getting ready for a career as a computer animator/by Bill Lund.
p. cm.
Includes bibliographical references and index.
Summary: Describes how computer animation has developed, its uses in various fields, and some related careers.
ISBN 1-56065-549-6
1. Computer animation--Juvenile literature. [1. Computer animation.
2. Computer animation--Vocational guidance. 3. Vocational guidance.]
I. Title.
TR897.7.L86   1998
778.5'347'028566--dc21
                                    97-12200
                                      CIP
                                       AC

Photo credits
Chuck Place, 4
Int'l. Stock/Scott Barrow, 6; Mark Bolster, cover, 18
Computer Associates, 8, 11
Archive Photos, 14, 17, 38, 44
FPG/12, 26, 34, 36, 43, 47; Arthur Tilley, 20; Mark Scott, 22
Unicorn Stock/Martin Jones, 25; Tom McCarthy, 30
Renco, 28
Silicon Graphics, Inc., 33

Table of Contents

Chapter 1 A World of Animation........................ 5

Chapter 2 History of Computer Animation 13

Chapter 3 Using Computer Animation 21

Chapter 4 A Career in Computer Animation 31

Words to Know 40

To Learn More 42

Useful Addresses 45

Internet Sites 46

Index 48

Chapter 1
A World of Animation

Some people think cartoons are just for fun. But cartoon animation is also used in many serious ways. Animation is a way of drawing cartoon pictures so they seem to move. Animation is used to sell things, to teach people, and for entertainment. Animators are the artists who create these moving cartoons.

Thirty years ago, all animation was done by hand with pen and paper. Today, many animators use computers to create animation.

Many animators use computers to create animation.

Computers used to be too expensive and not powerful enough. But now computers can do amazing things.

Entertainment

Computer animation is used to create moving pictures for video games, CD-ROMs, and computer programs. A computer program is a set of directions that tell a computer what to do.

Computer animation is used on the Internet. The Internet is a large network that connects many computers. A network allows people to share information.

Computer animation is also used on interactive television. Interactive television is a service that lets the viewer play games and shop by using a television set.

Animation is everywhere on television and in films. Computer animators make the cartoons children watch on television. They also make cartoons for movies and videos. Computers can be used to create whole cartoon films or to add details to regular movies.

Animators make cartoons that children watch on television.

Many businesses use computer animation.

Computers helped create animated details in eight of the top ten movies of 1995.

Business

Many advertisements on television use animation to sell products. Businesses may start with their logo then make it stretch, spin, or fly. A logo is a picture that helps people know about something. NBC uses a peacock for its logo. Computer animation lets the peacock walk around and spread its colorful tail feathers.

Businesses use animated videos to teach workers how to do their jobs. Many businesses need to use large numbers or lots of difficult information. They often use computer animation to make charts and graphs of that information more interesting. A graph is a picture that shows the connection between numbers or amounts of things.

Other Uses

Scientists often use computer animation to teach people. They can create models of volcanoes and earthquakes. A volcano is a mountain with vents where lava erupts. An earthquake is a sudden, violent shaking of the earth. Animation also is used to track changes in weather. It shows how clouds and storms move. Doctors use computer animation to study the inside of human bodies.

Computer animation is used to train airplane pilots and astronauts. Computers can create life-like flight situations. This helps beginning pilots practice their skills without the danger of actual flying.

People who build airplanes and space ships also use animation. They can test the effects of wind, speed, and gravity on a computer model. Gravity is the force that pulls things to the earth's surface and holds them there. Computer animation is much safer and cheaper than building models and having people test them.

Architects often use computer animation. An architect is a person who plans and draws buildings and houses. Animation shows how a building will look when it is finished. It can show the inside and outside of the building.

Lawyers hire animators to make videos of events that are important to trials. Computer animation might be used to show what happened in accidents or crimes.

Scientists use computers to draw maps of earthquakes.

Chapter 2

History of Computer Animation

W insor McCay created the first animated cartoon almost 90 years ago. It was called "Gertie the Dinosaur." Soon, Walt Disney and others also became interested in animation. They worked hard to add sound and make the cartoons look better. In 1937, Disney made his first full-length cartoon movie. It was called *Snow White and the Seven Dwarfs.*

Many people became interested in animation after Winsor McCay created the first animated cartoon.

Disney's movie was very popular. His success inspired other people to draw cartoons. In the 1950s, William Hanna and Joseph Barbera created many cartoon characters. Two of their most famous were the cat and mouse characters of Tom and Jerry. Tex Avery and Chuck Jones created Bugs Bunny. And Norman McLaren produced many animated cartoon films in Canada.

But using computers to create animation is very new. Companies like Bell Telephone and CBS Sports used computers in 1970 to create pictures for television. But computers were large and expensive to use. Only big companies could afford to use them.

In 1971, scientists figured out a way to make computers much smaller. This also made them cost less, so more people could afford them. People began looking for ways to play games and draw pictures on their computers. But most computer owners did not know much about making cartoon movies.

Tex Avery and Chuck Jones created Bugs Bunny.

One man who was good at using computers and making movies was George Lucas. He made *Star Wars*. He wanted to try using computers to create the special effects for his next movie. He wanted to create five jet planes flying together. His idea did not work, but it gave people ideas about other things to try.

Soon, computer animation was used in other movies. A green rock appeared to come to life in *Star Trek: The Wrath of Khan*. The first animated computer character was a knight made of stained glass. It appeared in the movie *Young Sherlock Holmes*.

Disney also began using computers in 1986 to create details in their movies. Disney movies were still created using traditional animation. But movies like *Beauty and the Beast* used computer-animated effects throughout the movie. One of the most amazing computer effects was a crystal chandelier with twinkling candles.

Walt Disney helped make animation popular. Disney Studios began using computer animation in 1986.

Animators tried many new things as computers became faster and more powerful. Finally, they were able to create whole television shows and movies on computers.

In 1994, a Canadian studio created a television series called *ReBoot*. The series uses only computer animation. Sixty animators work on powerful computers to make the popular show. It is seen every week in 47 countries.

In 1995, *Toy Story* became the first full-length movie animated entirely on computers. It was one of the most popular movies of the year. Using computers saved money making the film, but it still took a lot of time. Animators worked over 800,000 hours on computers to get everything just right.

Entire movies can now be created on computers.

Chapter 3
Using Computer Animation

Animation requires the skills of many people. It took 70 animators to make *Pocahontas* using traditional animation. But with the help of computers, only 27 animators were needed to make *Toy Story*. Computers have become a powerful tool for animators. Computer animators still come up with the ideas and plan for a project. Then computers help them do the rest of the work.

Toy Story was made on computers like this one.

Creating Characters

First, animators work with writers to decide which story they will tell. They design the characters and plan the setting. A setting is where and when a story takes place.

Animators can draw characters on paper. They can also use special computer programs to draw pictures on the screen. Animators have used computers to create dinosaurs, ghosts, talking animals, and dragons. The computers can show details like fur and feathers. Computer drawings of these creatures look just like photographs.

Storyboards

Second, special artists draw pictures that show the main parts of the story. This stage of the animation is called a storyboard. The storyboard looks like a giant cartoon strip in a newspaper. A storyboard for a long movie may have 4,000 or more drawings.

Animators can use special computer programs to draw on the computer.

Sometimes artists use computers to draw the storyboards. They draw with special pens on tablets that record the drawings and show them on the computer screen. Animators drawing storyboards on computers can make changes easily. The drawings can be put in a different order if the story changes.

In-betweening

Third, animators draw more pictures of the characters in action. Each animator works on a main section of the storyboard. Animators usually draw the main pictures by hand with pencil and paper.

Computers can figure out how much the character moves from one picture to the next. Then assistant animators draw pictures that show each tiny change of movement. This is called in-betweening.

Thousands of these drawings fit in between the main pictures. A long animated cartoon

---

Animators draw with special pens on computer tablets.

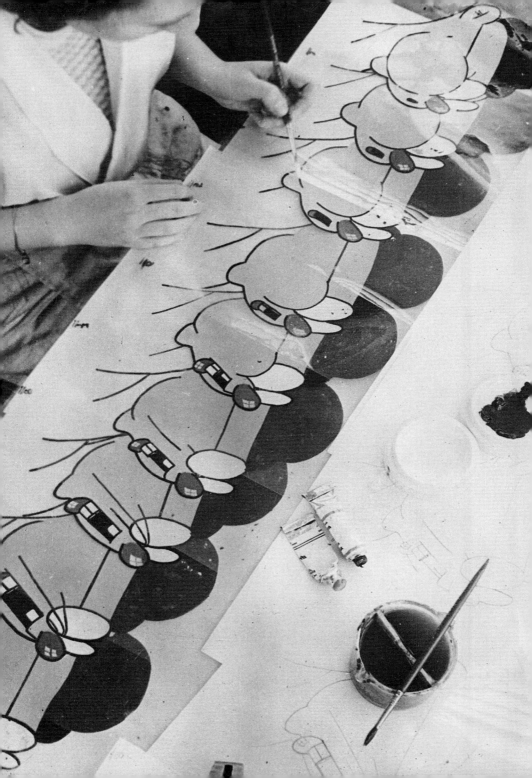

movie like *Hercules* or *Pocahontas* can take 500,000 drawings.

The pictures are put in order. The character appears to move when all the pictures are shown together at high speeds. It takes 24 pictures shown each second to make the character move smoothly.

Coloring

Next, a team of special artists colors in all the pictures. Each picture looks like a page in a coloring book. Artists working by hand can only color about 25 drawings a day. With a computer, they can color the drawings much more quickly.

Artists select a color from the computer's memory. Then they choose a small part of the drawing. The computer will fill in that part instantly with the selected color. The computer can color all the drawings the same. The coloring is even and exact.

Animators draw many pictures that show each tiny change of movement.

Special Details

Computer animators create many of the details in movies. Animators used computers to create the tornado in *Twister* and the river in *Pocahontas*. Animators can use computers to draw leaves on trees and add texture to a character's clothes. Texture is the look and feel of something. Computers can create shadows. They can change the way light appears to shine on an object. They can create lightning.

In *Jumanji*, animators created all of the movie's animals on computers. The details that made the animals seem real took a long time to create. Animators worked for years just drawing the hair in the lion's mane.

Animators use computers to create many special details in movies.

Chapter 4
A Career in Computer Animation

Animators must like to draw and paint. They must like to figure out how things move. Many times, animators have to try new techniques. They have to be good at solving problems.

In high school, future animators take art classes and computer classes. They save their best drawings and sketches in a portfolio. A portfolio is a folder of artwork that the artist shows to other people.

Future animators take art classes and computer classes.

Future computer animators need special training after high school. In the early 1980s, only a few schools trained people to be animators. Now, many technical and junior colleges offer classes in computer animation. A technical college is a school that offers hands-on training for particular careers. A junior college is a two-year school that offers complete programs or prepares students for further study.

About 50 schools in Canada and the United States offer degrees in computer animation. A degree is a title given by a college. A degree in animation takes one or more years to complete.

Most new animators work for a few months as interns. An intern is someone who is learning a skill or job by working with an expert. Animators start out doing coloring or drawing the in-betweens. Junior animators work on backgrounds or special details. Experienced animators plan projects, create characters, and draw storyboards.

New animators work for a few months as interns.

Today, animators must know how to use watercolor, pen and ink, and crayons. But many computer animators do most of their work on computers. The best training for these computer skills happens as animators work. Computers change so quickly that animators must learn on the job.

About half of all computer animators work for studios. A studio is where films, movies, or television shows are made. Other computer animators do freelance work. Freelance means working for more than one company. Freelance animators work for many companies and get paid separately for each project.

People just starting to work as a computer animator make about $18,000 each year. The average pay for all people who work in this field is $25,500 per year. Some senior animators make $100,000 or more a year.

Most animators today work on computers.

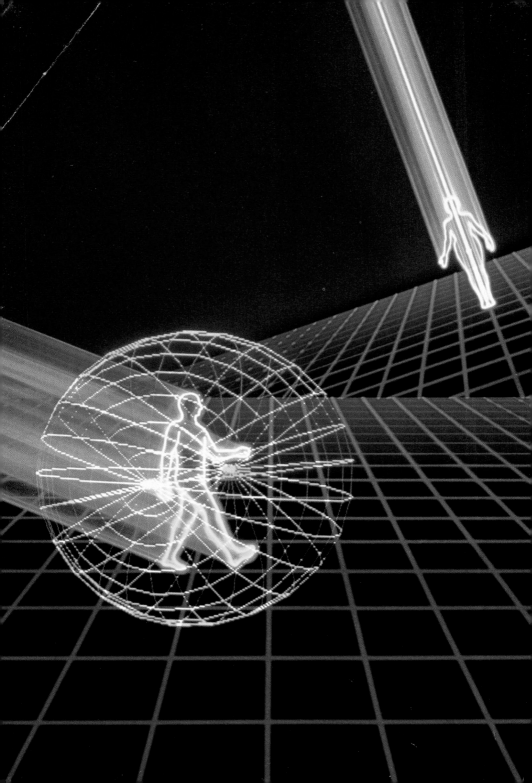

In The Future

The number of jobs for computer animators is increasing. People enjoy watching animation, and computer-animated films have been very successful. Animation is being used in more ways. Improved computers help animators entertain and teach people.

Computer animation began less than 30 years ago. It has grown quickly. Animators have discovered many amazing effects they can create with computers. They have many new ideas they would like to try. Computers are moving the art of animation in a new direction. Computer animators can look forward to an exciting future.

More and more uses for animation are being found.

Words to Know

animation (an-i-MAY-shun)—a way of drawing cartoon pictures so they seem to move

computer animation (kuhm-PYOO-tur an-i-MAY-shun)— a way of using computers to draw moving cartoons.

freelance (FREE-lanss)—a person who works for many companies and gets paid for each project

in-betweening (in-bi-TWEEN-ing)—the drawings that come in between the main pictures of the storyboard

intern (IN-turn)—someone who is learning a skill or job by working with an expert in that field

Internet (IN-tur-net)—a huge network that connects many computers

portfolio (port-FOH-lee-oh)—a folder of artwork to show others

storyboard (STOR-ee-bord)—a set of drawings that show the main action in an animated story

studio (STOO-dee-oh)—a place where films, movies, or television shows are made

texture (TEKS-chur)—the look and feel of something

To Learn More

Creating Animation on a Computer. Van
Nuys, Ca: AIMS Media, 1988.
Videocassette.

Johnson, Paul. *How to Draw and Paint
Cartoons and Animation.* Edison, NJ:
Chartwell Books, 1994.

Multimedia: The Complete Guide. New
York: DK Publishing, 1996.

Computer animation is used to track changes in weather.

MATT GROENING

Useful Addresses

Hanna-Barbera Cartoons, Inc.
3400 Cahuenga Boulevard
Hollywood, CA 90068-1376

International Association of Animated Filmmakers
ASIFA-Hollywood
725 Victory Blvd.
Burbank, CA 91505

Motion Picture Screen Cartoonists, Local 841
25 West 43rd Street
New York, NY 10036

Sheridan College
Schools of Communication Design
1430 Trafalgar Road
Oakville, Ontario, L6H 2L1
CANADA

Computer animators create many characters for television and movies.

Internet Sites

Disney.com Home Page
http://www.disney.com

Learn About Cartoons
http://www.cartooncorner.com/artsfolder/
  learningabout/animation.html

Welcome to Pixar's Home Page!
http://www.pixar.com

Welcome to Warner Bros. Animation!
http://www.wbanimation.com

Computers are moving the art of animation in many new and exciting directions.

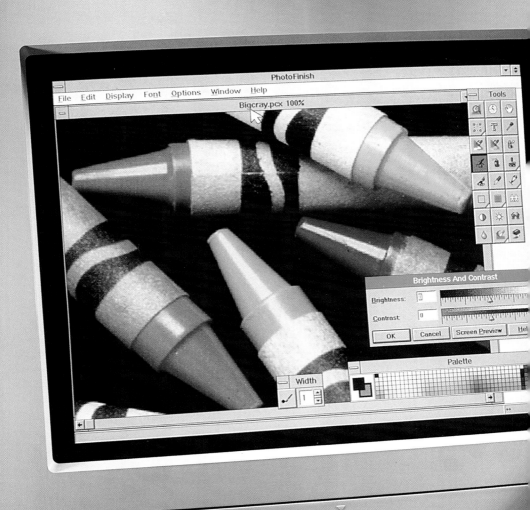

Index

advertisement, 8
Avery, Tex, 15

Barbera, Joseph, 15
Beauty and the Beast, 16
Bell Telephone, 15
Bugs Bunny, 15

cartoon, 5, 7, 13, 15, 23, 27
CBS Sports, 15
character, 16, 23, 24, 27, 29, 32
coloring, 27, 29
computer program, 7, 23

degree, 32
Disney, Walt, 13, 15, 16

entertainment, 5, 7

freelance, 35

"Gertie the Dinosaur," 13

Hanna, William, 15

Hercules, 27

in-betweening, 24, 27

Jones, Chuck, 15
Jumanji, 29

Lucas, George, 16

McCay, Winsor, 13
McLaren, Norman, 15

Pocahontas, 21, 27, 29
portfolio, 31

ReBoot, 19

Snow White and the Seven Dwarfs, 13
Star Trek: The Wrath of Khan, 16
Star Wars, 16
storyboard, 23-24, 32

Toy Story, 19, 21
Twister, 29